Decorative Painting
Zhostovo Style

DECORATIVE PAINTING
ZHOSTOVO STYLE

HEATHER REDICK, CDA

NORTH LIGHT BOOKS

CINCINNATI. OHIO

About the Author

Heather Redick is a world-renowned decorative artist and designer living in Ontario, Canada. Since 1990 she has owned and operated The Tole Booth, a decorative art retail store and mail order business.

She is a very popular teacher of Zhostovo-style floral painting throughout Canada, the U.S. and in Japan, and has recently begun conducting painting lessons via the Internet. She has also been invited to teach in Singapore, Malaysia, Venezuela and Portugal. A member of the National Society of Decorative Painters, she received her CDA certification in 1992.

Heather is the designer and author of five project books for Plaid Enterprises, over sixty instructional packets for decorative painters, and several magazine articles. She paints in both oils and acrylics, and has studied with the Russian master Larissa Dyatlova.

But by far, Heather's greatest joy is teaching. She has analyzed brushstroke techniques thoroughly, from the loading of the brush to the movement of the hands and shoulders, and loves to show students how easy it is to accomplish beautiful, rhythmic brushstrokes.

Other fine North Light Books are available from your local bookstore, art supply store or direct from the publisher.

03 02 01 00 99   5 4 3 2 1

Library of Congress Cataloging-in-Publication Data

Redick, Heather
    Decorative painting Zhostovo style / Heather Redick.
        p.   cm.
    ISBN 0-89134-968-5 (alk. paper).—ISBN 0-89134-987-1 (pbk. : alk. paper)
    1. Painting. 2. Folk art. 3. Decoration and ornament—Russia (Federation)—Zhostovo. I. Title.
TT385.R43 1999
745.7'23—dc21   99-24605 CIP

Editors: Dawn Korth and Kathy Kipp
Production Editors: Michelle Howry and Christine Doyle
Production Coordinator: Kristen Heller
Interior photography: Christine Polomsky
Designer: Wendy Dunning

❧ Dedication

This book is dedicated to my most creative of labors.

The greatest joy in my life has been to see my children grow to be healthy, prosperous people, each able to use their own God-given talents as they venture through life.

To my son Craig and daughter Kimberly—you are always in my thoughts.

❧ Acknowledgments

I would like to thank all those who have helped me through my years of painting with their advice, moral support and physical labor.

I want to mention Doreen Howard, who introduced me to my brush; Priscilla Hauser, who encouraged me to use it; and Larissa Dyatlova, whose masterful skills have shown me its potential.

To my husband, son and daughter, who support me and work with me to bring my goals closer to reality; my friend, Lynn Alderdice, who is never too far away when work needs to be done; and my co-worker, Percy Bedard, who tolerates my constant creative demands with a smile. I will always appreciate your understanding and devotion.

During the past few years, I have had the opportunity to work with many students. Their enthusiasm, patience, friendship and distinctive skills have given me motivation and been a constant source of knowledge. With their help, I have advanced my own abilities. I owe them a great deal of gratitude.

I wish to extend a very sincere thank-you to North Light Books for this presentation of my work. I am especially grateful to Heather Dakota, who first approached me about the possibility of doing this book, and to Kathy Kipp, whose enthusiasm, hard work and expertise have made it a reality.

ઝ Table of Contents

❧ Introduction ❧

As I watched Larissa Dyatlova paint those first few strokes and witnessed leaves and flowers coming into full bloom right before my eyes, I shivered with excitement. Would I ever achieve the understanding and skills to do this myself?

Russian artists studied for years to develop their painting skills. They learned from seasoned masters whose observations, knowledge and practice were based on perfecting the techniques of artists who had been painting for hundreds of years before them.

I tried to grasp all that I could during those few days with Larissa and knew the only way to achieve my new goal was to practice—and practice I have! As I continue to paint this style, I feel greater satisfaction. I know that if I continue to work hard, perhaps one day a student will stand over me as I paint and feel the same excitement I experienced when I witnessed the leaves and flowers in that beautiful bouquet come alive with color, movement and all of the rhythm intended by Mother Nature.

Zhostovo

The delicately intricate floral designs of the Zhostovo style of painting stemmed from the countryside of eighteenth-century Russia. Farmers and villagers of the Zhostovo region, outside of Moscow, began this unique form of folk art by painting traditional Russian scenes on everyday objects.

The techniques gradually changed to concentrate on floral bouquets and were applied to the growing tray-making industry that began in the early 1800s. What began as traditional Russian culture has evolved into a beautiful, recognizable contemporary art form.

About This Book

I have adapted the Zhostovo look using wonderful new products readily available on the market along with contemporary painting techniques. The instructions are written for acrylic and oil painters, and are intended to be used by artists of all skill levels. Detailed, illustrated steps will help you understand my methods and see the similarities between each flower and pattern. I hope that by showing you how I determine and arrange the elements of my painting, you will be encouraged to create your own designs.

It is important to read through and gain an understanding of the instructions before beginning to paint. This information is intended only as a guideline. There are no rules or restrictions. The Zhostovo technique allows for your own creativity and a free expression of color, movement and content.

Be aware that practice and perseverance will be your greatest assets. You've heard the saying, "If at first you don't succeed, try, try again," and I think that is particularly appropriate here. Be happy and proud of your creative successes but don't settle for what you accomplish. Always strive for more. Although my painting provides me with a great deal of contentment, I have yet to reach my own level of satisfaction. I hope that day never comes.

CHAPTER 1

Supplies

Brushes

You cannot paint well unless you have good tools to work with. That's especially true when painting in the Zhostovo style. Don't settle for less than excellent tools.

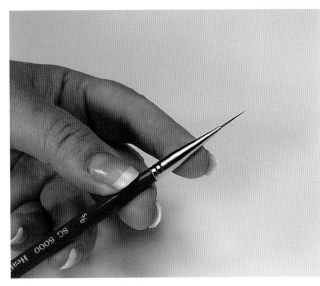

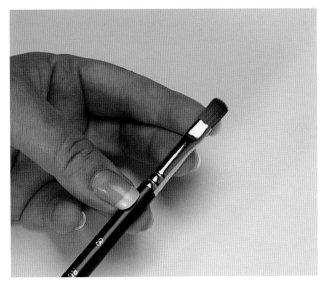

LINER BRUSHES

Execution of the fine, flowing liner work and building the delicate borders of the Zhostovo style requires a quality liner brush. It must hold a large amount of color and retain a fine point, yet when you apply pressure, it should create a more substantial line, leaving a uniform trail of paint. The liner brushes sold under my name give you the necessary control because of the handles' shapes, sizes and weight. The brush hair holds a tremendous amount of thinned paint and will facilitate a variety of deliberate lined effects, offering you more control than a script liner with longer hair. I use only three sizes (nos. 0, 3/0 and 5/0) for all of my work.

FILBERT BRUSHES

The traditional Zhostovo technique calls for round, natural hair brushes. I painfully struggled through my first floral tray using these brushes. You will discover that using filbert brushes will make it easier to paint this style when you're first beginning. Filbert brushes produce a curved outline to the beginning of your stroke and allow you the control of a flat brush. I choose sizes to suit the leaf or flower I am working on.

FLAT AND MOP BRUSHES

Floating and double-loading, techniques *not* used by the Russians, are most easily executed with a large flat brush. I also use these brushes for blending on the fruit before lightly dusting with a mop brush. Suitable quality flat brushes should offer enough thickness to hold a quantity of paint, provide a chisel edge and spread to at least double their width when called upon to do so. Flexibility, a soft feel, resilience and the ability to re-form to its original edge when pressure is released are other qualities you need to look for in a brush. Price does not necessarily guarantee quality.

SIZE SUGGESTIONS

I have been using the Expression line by Robert Simmons. The shape and balance of the handle appeal to me, and the brushes seem to do what *I* want them to do, not what *they* want to do. I prefer to use larger flats (¾-inch, ½-inch [1.9cm, 1.2cm], no. 12, no. 10, no. 8) and primarily the no. 8 filbert, sometimes moving down to a no. 6 or no. 4. The area you are working on determines the mop sizes. The ¾-inch, ½-inch and ¼-inch (1.9cm, 1.2cm, 64mm) brushes are useful sizes.

Paints

I love to work in oils and acrylics separately, and in combination with each other. I usually work with a limited palette in oils, but I've listed premixed colors to correspond with the acrylic paints for your convenience.

ACRYLIC/BLENDING MEDIUM

I use nontoxic FolkArt Artists' Pigments and FolkArt Acrylic Colors by Plaid because of their rich color and consistency. Acrylic color is available in squeeze bottles, tubes and jars. I find the bottles easier to work with and store, and I enjoy the wide range of premixed colors. They are also affordable.

Plaid has also developed a Blending Gel Medium that I use to simulate the wet-into-wet technique used by oil painters. Using the Blending Gel allows the paint to move freely, adding transparency but allowing each color to retain its own qualities.

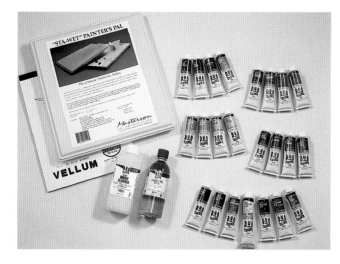

OILS/MEDIUM

Water-soluble oil colors eliminate the need for odor-producing solvents and provide for easy cleanup. Although water-soluble oil colors reproduce the characteristics of traditional oil colors, the drying time is reduced. By mixing this type of oil paint with your traditional oils, acrylics, watercolors or gouache, you can create exciting mixed media results. I work with Duo Aqua Oil (Holbein) colors. They offer eighty quality colors. Holbein also offers Duo Aqua Oil which I use in place of linseed oil as my blending medium. Another alternative is Painting Medium (Jellied), also by Holbein, which allows for transparency and faster drying but requires cleanup with conventional oil solvents.

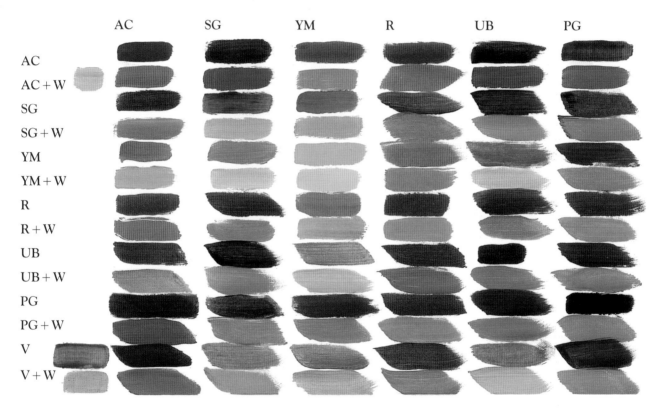

Mixing Color

As a general rule, I use only a limited oil palette of eight colors: Alizarin Crimson, Sap Green, Yellow Medium, Ultramarine Blue, Payne's Gray, Viridian, Red and White. This chart offers you a look at the range of colors that can be achieved by mixing these few colors.

HOW TO USE THIS COLOR MIXING CHART

1. Choose your base color, for example, Alizarin Crimson (AC), and find it in the left-hand column.
2. Choose the color you wish to mix with the AC, for example, Ultramarine Blue.
3. Find the Ultramarine Blue (UB) column by following along the top of the chart.
4. Find where the two columns intersect to see the approximate color you can expect.
5. If you wonder how it would appear as a lighter tone, use the same method and begin with a base color plus white; for example, Alizarin Crimson + White = AC + W.

Acrylic colors FolkArt Artists' Pigments		TCS #		Water-soluble oil colors Duo Aqua Oil (Holbein)
Pure Black 479		BK 5-1-8		Ivory Black 350
Sap Green 458		GR 8-3-9		Sap Green 244
Alizarin Crimson 758		RE 6-4-8		Alizarin Crimson 201
Payne's Gray 477		BL 4-9-9		Payne's Gray 336
Titanium White 480		WH 5-1-1		Titanium White 461
Medium Yellow 455		YE 4-1-5		Light Yellow 231
Red Light 629		RO 5-1-7		Vermilion 208
Burnt Sienna 943		BR 6-2-6		Burnt Sienna 318
Raw Sienna 452		BR 2-2-5		Raw Sienna 316
Prussian Blue 486		BL 5-2-7		Prussian Blue 273
Light Red Oxide 914		RE 4-6-5		Brown 310
Pure Magenta 689		RV 3-2-8		Mauve 295
Cerulean Blue 464		BL 7-2-8		Cerulean Blue 271

FolkArt Acrylic Colors

Teal 405		BG 4-1-7		Viridian 240 + White 461
Raspberry Sherbet 966		RE 6-5-5		Light Magenta 300 + Alizarin Crimson 201
Periwinkle 404		BV 5-4-8		Blue Violet 296
Peach Perfection 617		RO 2-3-3		Pink 216 + White 461 + Yellow 232
Strawberry Parfait 751		RE 4-3-6		Pink 216
Italian Sage 467		GR 3-8-4		Green Gray 333 + White 461
Hauser Green Medium 460		GR 7-4-5		Green Gray 333
Barnyard Red 611		RE 4-2-7		Rose Gray 330 + Brown 310
Charcoal Gray 613		BK 6-2-8		Monochrome 3 344
Heartland Blue 608		BL 5-7-7		Payne's Gray 336 + Prussian Blue 273 + White 461
Cappuccino 451		BR 2-3-3		Yellow Gray 331
Azure Blue 643		BG 3-1-6		Cerulean Blue 271 + White 461
Leaf Green 447		GR 3-5-5		Deep Green 247 + White 461
Inca Gold 676 or any metallic gold color				

Palette Colors

Understanding color theory can be an awesome task. Fortunately, you need *not* refer to any of these guidelines when choosing your color palette to paint this style. You may use and mix any colors you wish. There are no rules!

The colors used for the projects in this book can be changed or substituted at will. I have listed all of the colors I used to paint the projects in this book. All of these can be changed except for those specified for shading.

I have added True Color System (TCS) numbers for your convenience beside each acrylic color. The TCS identifier divides the complete color spectrum into fifteen color families. A two-character alphabetic abbreviation and a unique three-digit number identify all colors and mixes. Each number is based on a scale of nine variations and color class they represent. You can find complete information by writing to P.O. Box 496, Danville, IN 46122-0496, or access free demonstration software (http://www.trucolor.com).

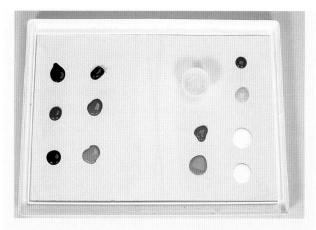

When I have chosen my colors, I organize my palette, leaving plenty of room for blending.

USING ACRYLICS

You cannot properly load your acrylic paint onto a synthetic brush on a surface that offers no "tooth," or has a slick finish. The Masterson paper offers the best blending surface for acrylics that I have found.

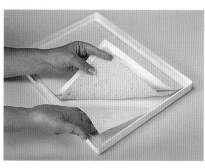

I soak this paper for at least twenty-four hours prior to its use and always have two or three prepared sheets under the wet sponge should I need them. Before I transfer useable paint to a clean sheet of prepared paper, I thoroughly rinse my sponge and palette case to avoid a stagnant buildup. I use my flexible, flat palette knife to move the paint to the clean sheet. I always rinse

the used paper in cold water and place it underneath the sponge. I reuse each sheet until it begins to allow more water through to the surface than I want. If I am not going to use the presoaked paper for some time, I allow it to dry. This preconditioned paper will need only five minutes of soaking the next time I use it.

When in use, I make sure that fresh cold water fills the sponge and touches the underside of the paper. The paper needs to feed from the water below, absorbing just the right amount to maintain the acrylic paint. Before organizing your paint colors on the palette, use a soft, absorbent towel to remove any excess moisture from the top surface. You do not want to add water to the paint and, in doing so, change its consistency; however, there are some dry, hot days when I need to gently "mist" the tops of the paint puddles. When I am traveling, I drain the water and leave the prepared paper under the damp sponge.

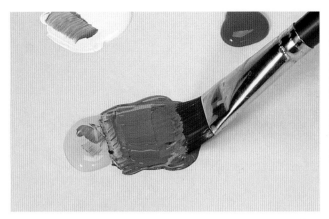

STORING AND BLENDING SURFACES

In addition to quality brushes and paints, you will need a surface suitable for maintaining paint consistency and for blending. I use two sizes of Masterson Sta-Wet Palettes—the large Pro for my acrylics and the Painter's Pal for my oils. Both have fitted lids to create a seal and my paint remains fresh for several days.

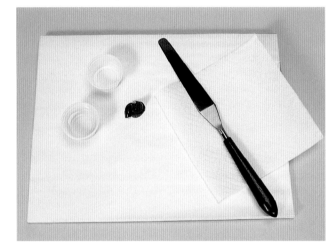

OIL PALETTE

The surface used for storing and blending your oil colors is also very important. With traditional tubed oils, as well as the water solubles, I use 9″ × 12″ (23cm × 30cm) sheets of tracing or vellum paper that fit and store nicely in the palette. These oils will stay useable for some time if left in the sealed palette. A light misting of linseed oil or solvent with some palette knife mixing might be needed to adjust the consistency.

Although I prefer not to use any aerosol spray paints or varnishes because of their airborne tendencies, it is more difficult to achieve a satisfying finish on dark backgrounds with brush-on products.

Your wax palette and other slick surfaces are great for mixing your acrylic and oil paints. When you have mixed your desired color or consistency, move this paint to your Masterson palette.

Additional Supplies

I have listed my personal preferences of brand names beside some supplies. If no name appears, any brand will suffice. The addresses for all of the suppliers are found in the Sources section at the end of the book.

- **Brush basin.** Choose a divided basin to separate clean water from dirty water, and one with ribs for help in cleaning brushes (Plaid Brush Basin).

- **Brush cleaner.** Brush Plus by Plaid works well to "cut" the acrylic in your brush. I use Duo Brush Cleaner when working with my water-soluble oils and Holbein Brush Cleaner "S" with my traditional oils.

- **Painting medium 0-530 (jellied).** This is another blending and glazing medium that can be used with traditional oil color or the Duo water-soluble colors.

- **Wet towels and alcohol.** I add a small bottle of alcohol to my wet towels to keep my hands and work area clean. The alcohol eliminates paint smears as you wipe.

- **Palette knife.** The knife should be flexible, strong and durable (Holbein No. Sl and Holbein SX Series No. 2).

- **Compass.** Your compass must have a fine, sharp point to secure it on wood surfaces.

- **Sandpaper and sanding block.** A variety of grits ranging from 80 to 1000 will come in handy.

- **Wood filler.** Some surfaces require touch-ups. Use a filler that is both stainable and paintable.

- **Kneaded eraser.** I like to knead two erasers together so that I have a larger, more manageable tool for removing pencil, chalk and transfer paper lines.

- *Transfer paper.* Choose a package that gives you both gray and white paper options, preferably 9″ × 12″ (23cm × 30cm) sheets.
- *Stylus.* Pick a double-ended stylus offering you a choice of fine and medium ball ends.
- *Strip palette.* A utility palette of waxed sheets is useful for mixing your acrylic and oil colors.
- *Tracing paper.* Either a large pad of tracing paper or tracing paper by the roll is useful especially for larger patterns.
- *Soft, absorbent towels.* Use flannel or a similar fabric if suitable paper towels are not available. Abrasive paper toweling will quickly ruin your brushes.
- *Ruler.* I prefer a 16″ (41cm) metal ruler.
- *Chalk pencil.*
- *Lead pencil.*
- *Tape.* Scotch Magic Tape is excellent for most uses.
- *Medium cup.* Bottle caps, small plastic cups or commercial palette cups are handy for your different paint mediums.
- *X-Acto knife.* The X2000 has a molded sponge rubber grip for better control when cutting around tricky shapes.
- *Spray mist bottle.* I keep two handy: one for water, and the other for my oil medium.

Extra Supplies for Specific Projects

- *Gold leaf and adhesive sizing.* Composition gold leaf in 4″ × 4″ (10cm × 10cm) sheets is easy to work with. Be sure to buy the appropriate sizing and use as instructed (Houston Art, Inc.).
- *Plastic wrap.* I use this to create mottled backgrounds.
- *Black spray paint.* Choose a matte finish paint specifically designed for use on metal.
- *Glass and tile medium.* (Plaid Glass and Tile Painting Medium.)
- *Glazing medium.* (Plaid Glazing Medium for acrylics.)
- *Glass cleaner.*

Sealing and Finishing Supplies

- *Matte varnish.* I prefer a water-based, nonyellowing product (Plaid Artists' Varnish Matte).
- *Wood sealer.* I used a mixture of 70/30 matte varnish to clear water.
- *Satin varnish.* If you prefer a subtle shine, choose a satin finish (Plaid Artists' Varnish Satin).
- *Gloss varnish.* (Plaid Artists' Varnish Gloss, brush-on FolkArt Clearcote Hi-Shine Glaze/Spray.)

Loading Your Brush

After you have prepared your palette and before you begin to practice the strokes illustrated, spend time learning how to load and control the paint in your brush. You need to become familiar with the "feel" of the paint consistency, the quantity of paint in your brush, the distribution of that paint and how it affects the reaction of the brush hairs.

In order to execute any brushstroke, first consider how the brush is to be loaded. Each stroke may be different, therefore, every time you load the brush may be different. You may require more or less paint and use a variety of consistencies. Always remember that you cannot achieve a desired stroke unless your brush is fully and evenly loaded with a predetermined quantity of paint.

LOADING ONE COLOR INTO YOUR BRUSH

Prepare your brush in the appropriate medium. If you are working with acrylic paint, use water. Oil brushes should be dipped in oil or solvent; brushes used with the water-soluble oil colors can be prepared in either.

Touch your wet brush to your absorbent towel to remove the excess medium. Do not rub your brush as this may damage the hairs. The absorbency of your towel, the pressure of your touch and the length of time that you press will determine how much moisture you remove. The amount of wet left in your brush will affect the consistency of the paint when you begin loading.

Flatten your brush on your palette. Do not alter the direction of the brush hairs. Pull paint into the bristles of the brush from one side of your puddle of paint.

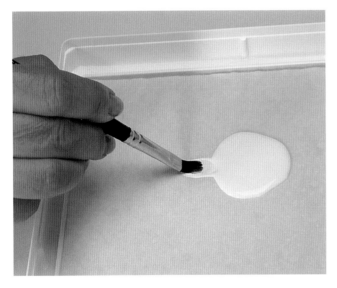

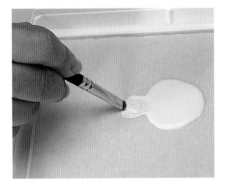

Repeat this, turning your brush over until you have ample paint *on* the brush.

Move to a separate section of your palette and work the paint into the bristles. Press, forcing the hairs to spread and contract. Continue this repeatedly until the paint is evenly distributed around each and every hair *within* the brush.

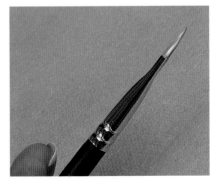

Replenish with paint and continue to blend until you feel it is fully and evenly loaded. Make sure not to change the shape, or chisel, on your brush.

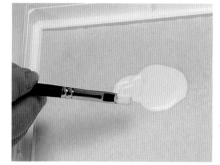  

If you load too much paint into your brush, do *not* rinse it and begin again. Simply wipe the flat outside hairs and excess paint on your towel and recoat from the blending area of the palette. Do not worry about getting paint up to, in or on the ferrule. Simply clean your brush well when you are finished with it.

SIDE-LOADING OR LOADING TO "FLOAT" COLOR

Prepare your brush in the appropriate medium. Touch your absorbent towel, removing most of the medium. Flatten your brush on your palette. Hold the brush upright so that the hairs spread.

Pull one side of the brush through the edge of your paint puddle. Be sure to pick up adequate paint.

Move to a separate portion of your palette and blend the paint into the brush.

Repeat the blending strokes on both sides of the brush. Be sure not to move the paint across and through the entire brush. Use your palette knife to keep the paint puddles neat to facilitate loading.

Loading your brush in this manner allows you to decide and execute the width of the float or side load that you want. For a narrow float, pull your brush through the outside edge of your paint puddle; for a wider float, move further into the puddle.

Always adjust the size of the puddle of paint to relate to the brush size you are using, for example, a large puddle of paint is required to load a large flat brush. A tiny puddle of paint is required to side-load a liner brush.

Working on a wet palette will allow you the necessary time for blending. A dry palette does not give you the "wet" time to properly blend.

LOADING YOUR LINER BRUSH

Wet your brush in your medium. Lightly touch your towel, leaving most of the medium in your brush. Lay your brush close to the palette and gently brush mix the medium, pulling paint from the edge of the puddle. Pull and turn without changing the natural direction of the brush hairs to create an ink-like consistency of color.

Continue to blend the paint into the brush, adding medium as needed and/or pulling paint into the mixture. The paint should flow easily and freely from the tip of your liner.

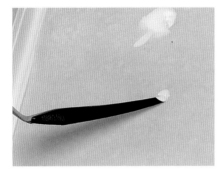

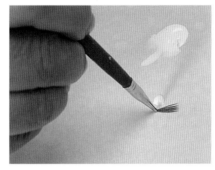

SIDE-LOADING YOUR LINER BRUSH

Use your palette knife to pick up a small amount of paint and move it to a clean spot on your palette, ensuring that the size of the paint puddle relates to the size of the brush.

Flatten the brush hairs on your palette.

Carefully pull the flattened hairs through the side edge of the puddle to the width you desire, and gently blend.

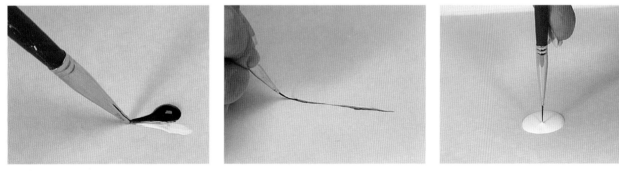

If you want to load two colors into your brush, simply pull the uncoated side through a similar tiny puddle of paint and gently blend. This technique is especially handy for small stems or any lines where shading one side would be desired.

LOADING YOUR LINER FOR DOT WORK

Prepare your liner in your medium. Touch your absorbent towel and remove almost all of the wetness. Touch the tip of the liner to the paint puddle, picking up the desired amount of paint.

CHAPTER 3
The Strokes

Creating a painting using a variety of strokes that relate to and work in combination with each other is exciting and rewarding. When you master brush control (strokes), you will paint with purpose and speed.

You must stop and think before doing each stroke. You need to understand that every angle change of the brush produces a different impression on your painted piece. Each movement of your fingers, wrist, elbow and shoulder changes the look of the stroke. Then add to this equation all of the paint varieties, consistencies, brush differences and quantity and distribution of paint in the brush. When you have considered these factors, then you are ready to proceed:

- Choose the proper size and type of brush for the desired stroke.
- Check the consistency of the paint. The longer and finer the

stroke, the thinner the consistency. For shorter, textured strokes, the paint needs to be creamier. For blended strokes, use an even bulkier consistency.

Look to see that the brush is fully and evenly loaded. If you are not satisfied with its appearance, return to your palette for further preparation.

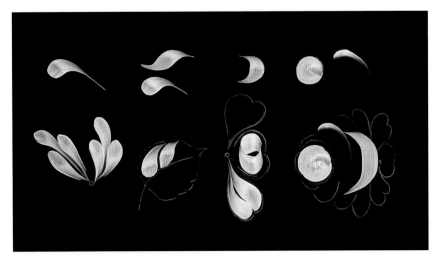

Make sure you are in a position that allows for free extension of your arms. Limit the use of your fingers and wrists by allowing your arm and shoulder movements to do the work.

Always approach your painting surface with the brush in a perpendicular position.

 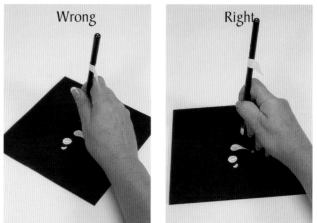

Decide where you want to start the stroke, and do not begin the stroke until you have determined where it is headed.

If you cannot clearly see the hairs of your brush, turn the surface and choose the best way to approach the stroke. You may *pull* toward yourself or *pull* away from yourself when executing a stroke, being careful that the hairs don't lose their intended shape. Your brush should slightly lean in the direction it is going.

FLAT STROKE

Load your filbert/flat brush thoroughly. With your brush perpendicular to the surface and the chisel at a 90° angle to the stroke direction, touch and then press down on the brush, causing the hairs to lie flat, and pull in a straight line. If you press into the stroke and hesitate, you will deposit paint on the surface.

This is the first stroke used in some flowers.

Pull the stroke to the desired length, or press and lift off, leaning your brush away from the direction it is headed, which creates a "wisping off" effect.

If you have neglected to attain a high level of competence with your strokes, you are not painting to your potential.

COMMA STROKE

To decide the angle on which to begin your stroke, determine where the stroke is headed and line the chisel edge of your brush up to that point.

Position your fully loaded brush perpendicular to your piece with the chisel or straight flat edge pointing to where your stroke is headed. When practicing, place a dot to help guide your stroke.

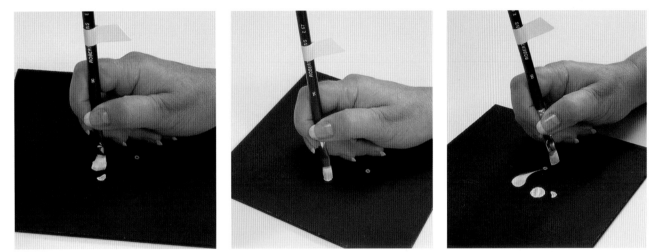

Touch and then press, allowing ample time for the brush hairs to spread. This will form the round end of your stroke and, depending on the pressure you apply, will determine the degree of fullness of the stroke.

Gradually and evenly lift and pull in one fluid motion toward your destination, leaning slightly into the gentle curve. Do not turn your brush or stray too far from your line of direction. As you lift off of the surface, your brush should have re-formed to its original point or chisel. You may need to lean the brush slightly back to cause the hairs to pull up, forming a fine tail.

If you don't decide where you are headed, you won't know what angle to begin your stroke with. When you practice, never produce rows and pages of meaningless strokes. Always choose a destination point. Paint your strokes from a variety of beginning spots with all of them converging at the same point. This way your strokes will relate to each other, and you will begin to understand that each stroke is slightly different

| 1 | 2 | 3 |
| Touch | Press | Pull and lift |

from its neighbor because it begins on a different angle.

UNFINISHED COMMA OR WISPED COMMA

In the pieces I have designed for this book, this stroke is used the most. It is executed in the same manner as a regular comma except that you must lift off, in a "wisping" motion, before finishing the stroke. To do this, lean the brush away from the direction you are moving as you lift off.

Comma   Shortened or Wisped Comma   Shorter Wisped Comma

SIDE-LOADED COMMA

There are occasions when you will need to execute a stroke with your brush side-loaded with paint. The stroke takes on a very different look, depending on whether the paint spreads to the inside or outside of the stroke.

Inside Float

Outside Float

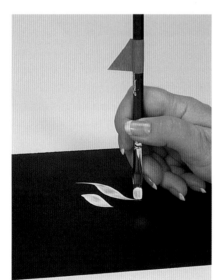

S STROKE

Although this stroke takes on the look of an **S** when it is finished, its shape is a result of the applied pressure in the middle of the stroke. It is not created by outlining an **S**. Line the chisel edge of the brush up with the destination of the stroke. Begin on the chisel edge, applying increased pressure as you move through the stroke. You must lean to one side or the other as this pressure is applied, making sure that the hairs of the brush follow and retain their intended shape. As you approach the last one-third of the stroke, lift up and allow the chisel edge of the brush to re-form. Your brush should not turn. The chisel begins, moves and ends on the same angle.

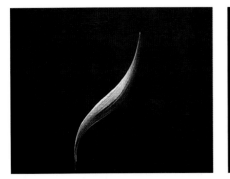

When you have mastered the **S** stroke, practice painting only the center of the stroke, without the beginning and end. Practice wisping off of the end of the stroke. The photo on the left shows a completed **S** stroke, and one with the middle only.

SIDE-LOADED **S** STROKE

Load only one side of your brush and paint a complete **S** stroke.

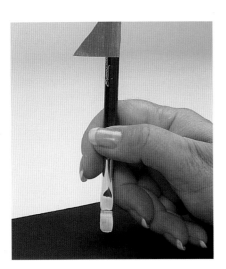

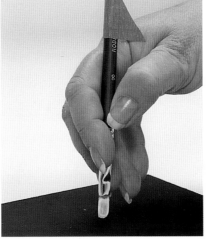

FILLED-IN CIRCLE

Position your brush to begin the stroke.

Create a coil by rolling the brush handle far enough back to force your wrist to follow.

When you have wound your wrist to approximately 360°, set the brush on your surface and begin painting. Touch, press and unwind slowly.

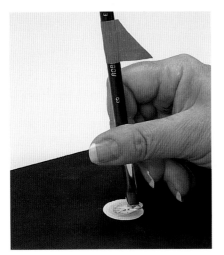

This is how the completed stroke should look.

Leave time for the hairs to regroup, rolling the handle back to its starting position and beyond.

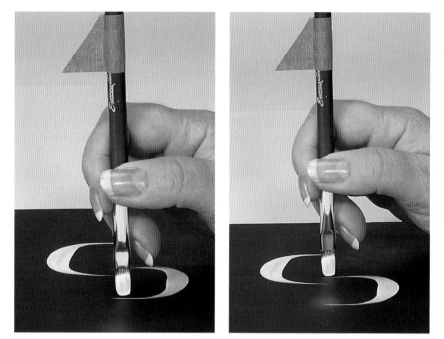

Create a variation on this by hesitating and applying a little extra pressure to the middle of the stroke or by side-loading your brush.

C STROKE

Carefully begin and end this stroke on the chisel edge of your brush. As you slowly move through its rounded shape, apply pressure to the center of the stroke.

LINER BRUSHSTROKES

You can achieve a wide variety of useful strokes with your liner by pulling it at varying speeds, applying pressure at different times, using a variety of consistencies of paint and changing its angle. Combine liner strokes to create beautiful borders.

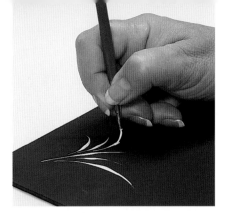
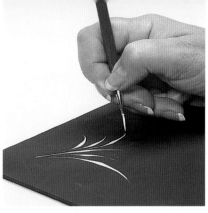
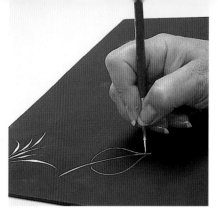

BOUQUET FILLER STROKES

Load your brush with a loose consistency of paint. Hold the brush perpendicular to the surface. Touch and pull in a straight or gently curved direction. Press, hesitate and allow the hairs to spread.

Resume moving through the stroke, giving the brush time to re-form to its point, and lift off.

VEINS

Load your brush with a loose consistency of paint, and hold it perpendicular to your surface. Do not apply much pressure as you pull from the stem into the leaf. Always paint a curved line. Release pressure as you move through the stroke, creating a diminishing fine line.

DOTS

Use your liner rather than the end of your stylus to create dots. Gently dab the very tip of the brush to the surface. For tiny dots, apply less pressure with a lightly loaded brush, and for larger dots, apply more pressure with a generously loaded brush.

ELONGATED COMMA

Load your brush with a thin consistency of paint. Touch, press, pull and gradually lift to the desired length of the stroke.

LINER LEAVES

Load your brush with a creamy consistency of paint. Lay the brush on its side. Touch the surface and pull (or push) without turning the brush. Gently raise the brush as you move.

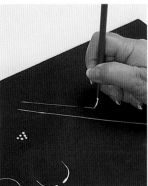

CURVED TEARDROP

Load your brush with a thin consistency of paint. Pull the tip of the brush in a curved shape, maintaining a light pressure. To finish, press, stop and carefully lift off.

STRAIGHT LINES

Load your brush with a thin consistency of paint. Position the tip of the brush at the beginning of the line. Pull the stroke with your shoulder and arm, making sure not to move your fingers or wrist.

CHAPTER 4

Surface Preparation and Finishing

I have used a variety of surfaces for the projects in this book, all of which require minimal preparation.

WOOD

Six of the projects were designed on wooden surfaces. Before starting, fill any imperfections with wood filler, and when dry, sand each piece smooth.

Seal each piece. Prepare a mixture of 50 percent matte varnish with 50 percent of the background color.

When dry, resand with a finer grade of paper (320 or finer). Apply at least two even layers of background color over the surface, lightly sanding between coats if necessary.

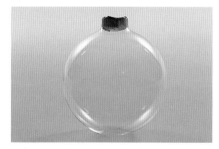

GLASS

Clean the glass with vinegar or glass cleaner of your choice. Then use a large flat brush, fully and evenly loaded with glass and tile medium, to frost the surface. Apply a coat without going over your strokes.

Note the angle and spread of the brush.

Allow a day for drying before covering it with your background color.

METAL

Clean the pie keeper with vinegar and water. Dry and spray it with two light, even coats of black matte metal primer. Brush on the background basecoat color. Always remember to use aerosol spray paints and varnishes outdoors.

Preprime the tray. Sand lightly if needed and coat with an even coverage of background basecoat color.

SPECIAL BACKGROUND EFFECTS

The metal tray was prepared with a mottled background behind the floral bouquet.

To achieve this look, basecoat with black around the outside rim and Cerulean Blue in the center. Apply an 80/20 black paint/water mixture over the blue. Lay plastic wrap over the wet surface and pinch it in different directions, pulling your spread fingers together. Allow the wrap to sit for a moment, then lift carefully. Let the paint dry and coat with a thin layer of matte varnish.

GOLD LEAFING

The birdhouse features gold leafing. Prepare your wood surface. Use Light Red Iron Oxide, Burnt Sienna or a similar color under the leafing. Apply a generous coat of gold leaf sizing to the desired area. Note that it is extremely adhesive. Allow this to dry.

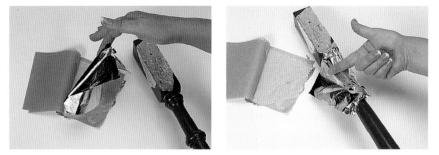

Pick up a sheet of gold leaf by touching it with a moist finger. Lay it over the glued area and smooth it with your fingers. Allow the background color to peek through the cracks in the leafing for a more aged look.

Smooth out the gold leaf with your fingers and buff smooth with a soft cloth. Save any remnants for future use.

TRANSFERRING PATTERNS

Trace the pattern onto a sheet of tracing paper. Position it on the prepared surface, and tape it securely at the top of the pattern. Then slip the transfer paper under the tracing. Choose a color that will easily show up on the background basecoat color. Use a pencil or stylus and retrace the pattern lines, making sure to press lightly. Check your transfer regularly. When transferring to a rounded surface, slice your tracing from the outside toward the center several times. Secure it at the top, and press the area to be traced down with your finger.

FINISHING YOUR PIECES

Brush on several coats of varnish, sanding lightly between coats with 400 or finer sandpaper. A gloss finish tends to bring out the color with black backgrounds, but certainly a satin or matte finish could be used if you prefer. The ornament finishes nicely with a spray glaze.

CHAPTER 5

Building Your
Own Bouquet

Understanding the formation of the leaves and flowers,
taking the time for some stroke practice and learning
some general guidelines for placement are all you need
to design your own wonderful creations.

To simplify the process, start by as-
sessing the surface you chose for the
design. Use the shape of the piece to
guide your development of the shape,
size and placement of the flowers and
leaves. Begin by drawing guidelines
to direct your eyes and hands.

If you are working on a round surface, trace the outside shape of the
piece onto tracing paper.

Then fold this tracing in half as many times as possible.

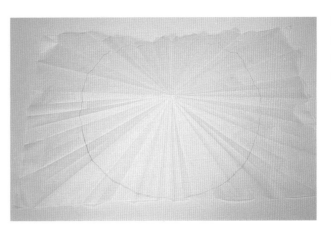

Unfold the paper
and use a ruler to
draw lines on the
creases.

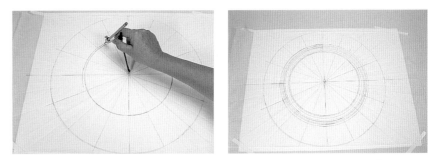

Using a compass, draw several circular lines to create a grid pattern.

Cut out the full circle and fasten it securely to the piece. Then slip some transfer paper under the tracing and pattern the surface.

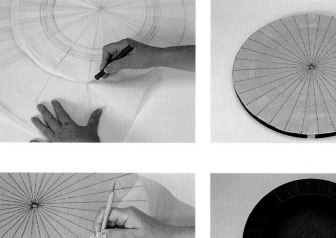

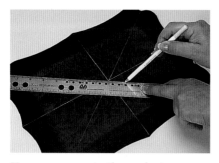

You can use a similar technique on a surface like this scalloped tray. Take advantage of the shape of the piece: the scalloped rectangular edge and the inside rectangle. Draw lines from point to point, from recess to recess and from corner to corner. This will pinpoint the center and balance the radiating lines.

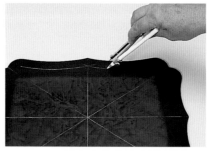

Use a compass to mark several lines around the outside edge, varying the distances between each. Use the compass and follow the inside rectangular shape for yet another set of guidelines.

These lines will help you with the placement of the leaves and flowers. Draw an uneven number of rough circles in the area around the center. These circles will be the flowers.

The radiating lines guide the placement of the leaf shapes.

After roughing in the shapes for the flowers and leaves, mark a spot on each flower just below the center. This mark acts as the guide or spot to which all of the strokes will be directed. It separates the back or top of the flower from the front or bottom, which usually faces the center of the bouquet. The first stroke of the flower is pulled from the center of the bouquet to the dot. This will be the bottom center of the flower.

Kissing **C** strokes could also be used to create this first shape. Be sure to press into each stroke to give it shape.

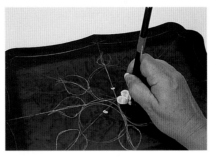

The second stroke tucks in on one side of the first. At this stage pay special attention to the beginning angle of the brush. Line up the chisel edge so that it is in a direct line with the "dot." Move the stroke directly toward this guide.

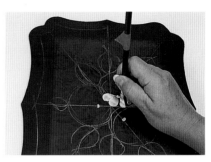

Tuck the third stroke on the opposite side of the center in a similar fashion.

Continue stroking from side to side, up and around each side of the flower, always directing your stroke to the original dot but not necessarily completing or continuing the stroke to that point.

Finish the top or back shape of the flower.

Fill in the center shape, in this case, an open mum. Begin in the middle of the center and pull the stroke toward the dot.

Work from side to side, filling in the center strokes.

The second flower shows the first stroke beginning in the middle of the flower center. Pull this stroke toward the dot. Add second and third strokes, working from side to side of the center.

Turn your piece as you form the back and top of this center. The brush should be at a right angle to the dot. Touch, then press and slowly tuck a comma-like stroke around the stroke beneath it. Do not change the angle of the brush through the stroke. Complete an outside shape that is similar to the first flower.

Begin the third flower. Use kissing **C** strokes to create the bottom center petal. This flower center is left open with no center strokes. All three flowers are constructed in a similar fashion, only varying the shape of their centers.

Fill in the leaf shapes with as few strokes as possible. This requires pressing into the brush for fullness. Begin with a comma stroke and then tuck in one or two S-like strokes. Note that my brush is directed toward the end of the leaf.

Finish the leaf shape with one or two comma and/or S strokes. Fill in the bouquet with smaller leaves or buds.

As you can see, creating a pleasing shape for your bouquet and arranging the leaves and flowers is not difficult. Following the guidelines for brush-strokes and their direction will allow you the freedom to design your own pieces.

CHAPTER 6

❧ *Creating Leaves* ❧

I have designed the finished pieces in this book using a couple styles of leaves. Once you have practiced and mastered these styles, you will find that creating variations is a simple matter. Before you begin to paint, read through the captions and carefully study the step-by-step illustrations. If you are working in acrylics, be sure to allow the paint to dry between every step from 2 through 8. If you choose to work with oils, allow time for drying between steps 2, 3 and 4. Steps 4 through 7 can be done wet-into-wet.

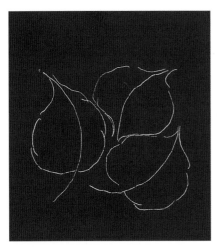

1 Transfer your pattern.

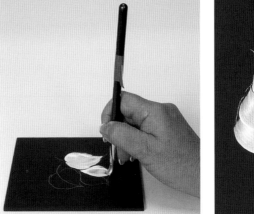

2 Undercoat with white using as few strokes as possible to fill in the leaf space.

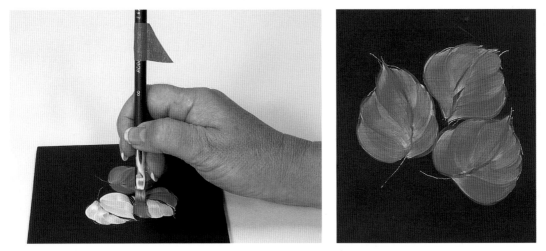

3 Basecoat with the color of your choice, being sure to cover all of the white. Raw Sienna was used for this illustration.

4 Side-load a large flat brush with Alizarin Crimson—the first shadow color. Float color from the convex side of the curved vein out, creating a dark side of the leaf. It doesn't matter which side you choose to be light or dark.

5 Add Alizarin Crimson to the bottom half or end of the leaf. *Note*: More shadow is better than less shadow.

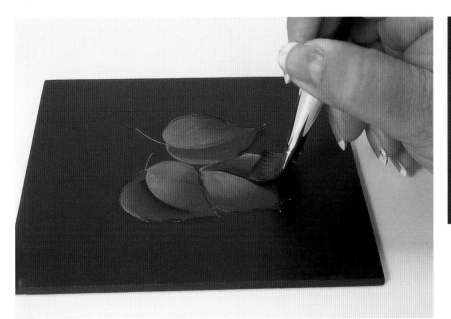

6 Deepen and emphasize the curved vein shape with Payne's Gray—the second shadow color—being sure that you can now see plenty of both shadow colors.

7 Deepen the shadow on the end of the leaf with Payne's Gray. Up to this step, completing the leaves can be easily accomplished, but the following steps are more difficult as you build the color, contrast and shapes of the leaves by painting strokes using a wet-into-wet technique. If you choose to use acrylics, you must be totally prepared before you begin step 8 because your paint and medium will dry quickly. You should not go over a stroke. You have the advantage of time when using oils, which are more forgiving if you choose to go over a stroke. *It is very important that you do not reload your brush with paint, or touch your water or oil medium once you begin the overstroke steps.* Wipe excess paint and medium picked up by the brush onto your soft, absorbent towel between strokes.

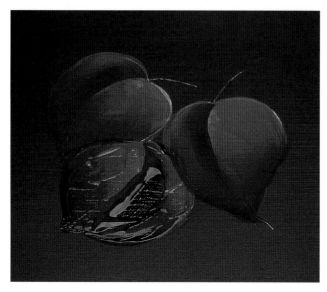

8 Coat the leaf with an even coat of medium. Use the Blending Gel Medium with acrylics as illustrated above, or a *thin* coat of linseed oil (Aqua Oil for water-soluble paints) or painting medium.

9 Cover the leaf with the shadow colors and original basecoat color. Acrylic painters need to pay attention to the large amount of wet paint on the leaf as shown in the illustration. Oil painters require far less wet color.

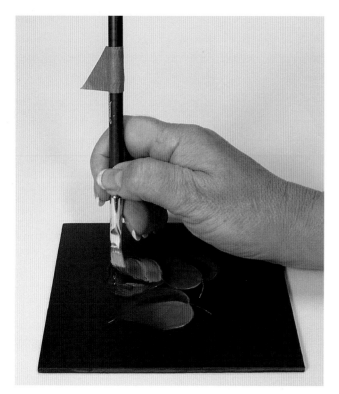

10 Prepare your brush with the first overstroke color, which is any tone slightly lighter than the basecoat color. A little white was added to Raw Sienna in this illustration. Begin with a comma stroke on the lightest top side of the leaf at the vein. Pull out and toward the end of the leaf. Do *not* finish the stroke, but rather, wisp off the end into the wet shadow color. Do not reload your brush. Fill in below with an unfinished **S** stroke. Tuck in another stroke if necessary.

Acrylic painters should prepare their brush with the overstroke color before beginning step 9.

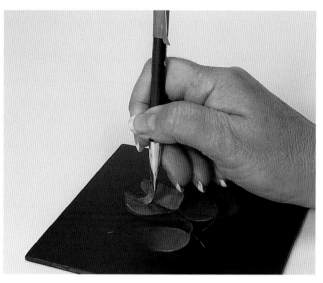

Pull flat, gently curved strokes from the outside edge of the dark side of the leaf, back up and in toward the vein. Begin at the top of the leaf and work down, still painting into wet shadow color. As you move through the strokes, you will pick up wet shadow color. Each progressive stroke will automatically become darker.

You may apply as many layers of strokes as you wish, lightening and adding color as you go and always painting wet-into-wet.

While the first layer of strokes is still wet, slightly lighten your overstroke color again and add a second layer of strokes. Begin these strokes at the vein line on the light side of the leaf. Do not necessarily go over the original strokes. Begin to add more shape and contrast. You may only need to add one or two strokes on the light and/or dark side of the leaf. Be very careful not to make the entire leaf the same degree of color.

While the second layer of strokes is still wet, slightly lighten your overstroke color again and add one or two highlight strokes.

11 Erase any pattern lines that may be showing. Add very fine lines to outline the shape of the leaf. The color of these lines should blend with the leaves.

12 Acrylic painters may wish to reestablish the shadow areas. Sap Green was used in this illustration, picking up the background color behind the leaves. Use this or either of your shadow colors.

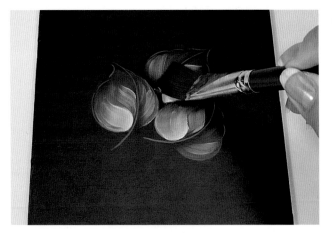

13 You may wish to separate a grouping of leaves by floating a shadow between them.

14 Fill in between leaves and flowers with liner leaves that follow the direction of the leaf shapes.

The following leaf is painted using the same steps.

1 Pattern.

2 Undercoat. Build the strokes in groups.

3 Basecoat.

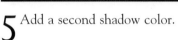

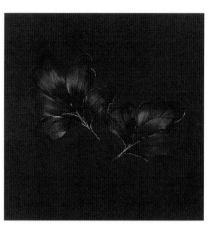

4 Add the first shadow color.

5 Add a second shadow color.

6 Begin the wet-into-wet painting technique. Coat with the medium and the shadow colors.

7 Add a first layer of strokes, following the shape of the leaf.

8 Add a second layer of strokes and then a third, creating contrasts and highlights.

9 Erase any pattern lines that are showing. Define the shape of the leaf with fine linework.

ers, Centers,

l and Fruit

similar to those for the leaves.
so a continuity of technique. Read
ations.

The Chrysanthemum

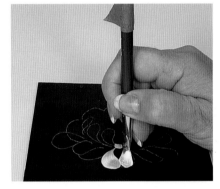

1 Transfer your pattern. You will need the outline as well as an indication of the flower center shape.

2 Undercoat the flower with white. Place a dot of paint to guide the angle and direction of your stroke. Begin in the middle of the bottom of the flower and pull your strokes toward the important dot. Be sure that the chisel edge of the brush is in line with the dot.

3 Build the outside shape of the flower, working from side to side and up and around to the back or top.

You can group your petals to create different and interesting flower shapes. You can add and vary strokes to create open and closed centers.

4 Basecoat with the color of your choice. Periwinkle was used in this illustration.

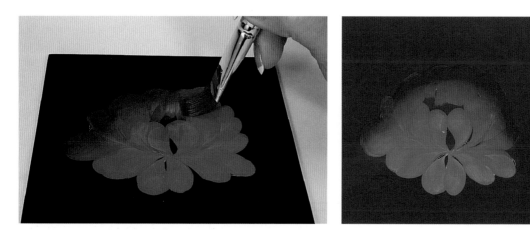

5 Side-load a large flat brush with Alizarin Crimson. Cover the back or top of the flower with a substantial shadow.

6 Deepen the shadow in and around the bowl center with Payne's Gray. Note that you can use Alizarin Crimson as well.

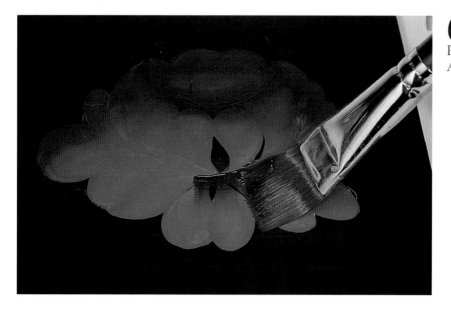

7 Deepen the shadow and broaden it by flipping your brush and floating more color to meet the first application.

8 Begin the wet-into-wet application of the overstrokes. Apply an even layer of medium to the flower. Cover the medium with the shadow colors and basecoat color in the appropriate areas. Use plenty of paint when working with acrylics as illustrated here. Use much less when working in oils.

9 Apply your first layer of overstrokes using a color slightly lighter in tone than the basecoat color. A little white was brush mixed with Periwinkle in this illustration. Do not reload your brush or touch your medium during this step. Continue to paint the strokes into the wet shadow, causing each progressive stroke to become darker. Paint the strokes in the order that was outlined in chapter five, "Building Your Own Bouquet."

10 Add a second and third layer of strokes slightly lightening the color between layers. Begin in the middle bottom of the flower and add strokes only as needed for contrast. You may not have more than one layer in the back of the flower, while the front and center may have two or three layers.

11 If your strokes do not offer enough contrast, you can highlight by floating light color on the tips of a few of the middle and bottom center petals. You may also float an S-like stroke on a few of the petals to exaggerate a flowing shape.

12 Add further contrast by slightly deepening the shadowed areas.

13 Erase any pattern lines that are showing. Highlight with fine linework. You may choose to use a little or a lot of linework to emphasize the shape of a stroke that is particularly appealing, or to change the shape to enhance the look.

14 Add the center to your flower. See "Flower Centers" on page 68 for more details.

The following flowers are painted using the same steps.

The Daisy

1 Transfer the pattern.

2 Undercoat.

3 Basecoat.

4 Add shadow to the center of the flower.

5 Add shadow to the back or top of the flower.

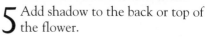

6 Deepen the center area with a second shadow color.

7 Begin the wet-into-wet over-stroke technique. Cover with your medium, wet shadow colors and basecoat color. Pull in the first layer of strokes in a color slightly lighter in tone than the undercoat.

8 Add a second and perhaps a third layer of highlight strokes.

9 Erase any pattern lines that are showing. Outline and add the center.

The Poppy

1 Transfer the pattern.

2 Undercoat.

3 Basecoat.

4 Add the first shadow color to the flower middle, top and back.

5 Deepen the shadow in the center.

6 Begin the wet-into-wet technique. Apply medium, shadow colors and basecoat color. Add the first layer of strokes using a color lighter in tone than the base coat.

7 While wet, add a second and perhaps a third layer of highlight strokes, slightly lightening the color each time.

8 Highlight the front petal with a float of light color.

9 Erase any pattern lines. Add the linework and flower center.

The "Five-Stroke" Flowers

1 Transfer the pattern.

2 Undercoat.

3 Basecoat.

4 Shade the flower tops and backs.

5 Deepen the shadow in the center.

6 Begin the wet-into-wet over-stroke technique.

7 Erase any pattern lines. Outline. Add the flower center.

Changing just the center can substantially vary the look of a flower.

The Apple Blossom

This flower is a variation of the previous "five-stroke" flower. Instead of using one stroke for each petal, two straight, comma-like strokes are grouped together.

1 Transfer the pattern.

2 Undercoat. No basecoat color was used. Instead, I worked with the white undercoat.

3 Shade the backs and tops of each blossom.

4 Deepen the shadow in the center.

5 Begin the wet-into-wet technique, using single overstrokes instead of doubled-up strokes for the petals.

6 Erase any pattern lines. Outline with an M-shaped pattern and add centers to the blossoms.

The Early Chrysanthemum

1 Transfer the pattern.

2 Undercoat, beginning with the center to guide the outside shape of the flower.

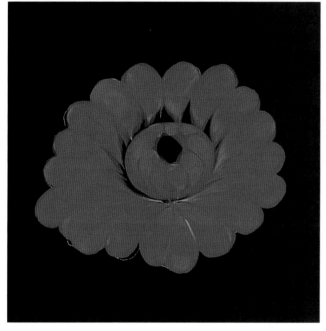

3 Basecoat.

4 Add shadow color to the back, top and around the center.

5 Deepen the shadow around the center.

6 Begin the wet-into-wet technique. Add your first layer of overstrokes.

7 Add a second and third layer of highlight strokes. Finish the outside petals before doing the center.

8 Still wet-into-wet, add the strokes to create the flower center bowl.

9 Erase any pattern lines. Outline and add the center. Refloat shadow colors around the bowl and flower back if more contrast is needed.

The Gardenia

1 Transfer the pattern.

2 Undercoat. Begin this flower the same way as the chrysanthemum. Fill in the bottom layers of petals after the initial shape has been established.

3 Basecoat.

4 Add the first shadow color around the top and back of the flower, as well as between the bottom layers of petals.

5 Deepen the shadow in the center and between the layers of petals.

6 Begin the wet-into-wet overstroke technique. Starting at the very bottom of the flower, add your first layer of overstrokes.

7 Build contrast by lightening your paint color as you advance through the petal layers. Reload your brush and begin in the middle of each layer, but do not reload as you work up and around to the very back of the flower.

8 Add a second layer of strokes for highlight.

9 Erase any pattern lines. Outline and add the center.

The Rose

1 Transfer the pattern.

2 Undercoat. Use full, sweeping **U** strokes to fill in the center.

3 Basecoat with color.

4 Add the first shadow color to the top or back and around the center bowl.

5 Deepen the shadow inside and around the bottom of the bowl.

6 Begin the wet-into-wet technique, building layers of strokes only around the bottom of the flower.

7 Finish the bottom of the flower with highlight strokes.

8 Side-load your brush with the lightest color. Pull a floated comma stroke from the side petals in toward the middle of the bowl and around the open bowl edge. Add short, faintly colored strokes inside the top of the bowl for the suggestion of petals.

9 Float a **U**-shaped stroke around the bottom of the bowl. You may need to go over this two or three times, making sure it fades gently into the background color.

10 Load your liner with a large amount of paint. Loosen the consistency only slightly. Lay the liner to its side and carefully roll the paint off of the brush, creating an uneven deposit. Pull toward the bottom edge of the floated comma until it connects and gently disappears into that edge. Repeat from side to side.

11 Erase any pattern lines. Outline and add the center.

The Bird

1 Transfer the pattern.

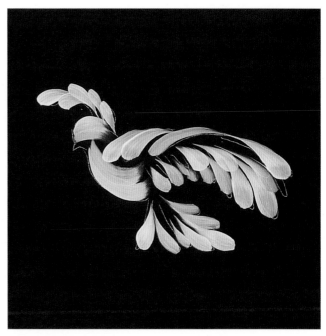

2 Undercoat with comma-like strokes, leaving open, unpainted space.

3 Basecoat with color, then add the shadows and deepen.

4 Begin the wet-into-wet technique. Add the first layer of strokes.

5 Add contrast with a second and third layer of strokes.

6 Add interest with different-colored overstrokes.

7 Use shortened, flat strokes to suggest feathering.

8 Erase any pattern lines. Outline, giving shape to the bird's beak and body. Add a dot for the eye.

Flower Centers

Centers can be as simple as using one dot of color, or as elaborate as using several steps, contrasts and colors. The following are suggestions for centers.

Poppy Center

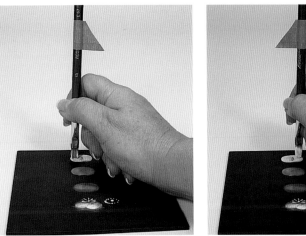 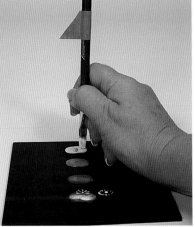 

1 Undercoat using kissing **C** strokes.

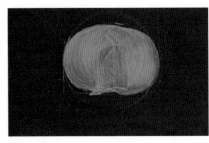  

2 Basecoat with color. I mixed a little yellow with Sap Green.

3 Add an Alizarin Crimson shadow to the top and a Payne's Gray shadow to the bottom of the shape.

4 Place a dot of color in the top center and pull straight, comma-like strokes in toward this dot. You could use a grouping of dots to form an oval shape.

Open Chrysanthemum Center

1 Use your filbert brush to create an arched shape by simply touching the surface, then lifting. I used a little yellow mixed with Sap Green.

2 Continue to build a mound of strokes, changing the angle of your brush with each touch to the surface.

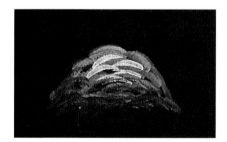

3 Highlight the top of the mound with a lighter color, adding white, yellow or both. Shade the bottom of the mound with Alizarin Crimson and Payne's Gray.

Daisy and Chrysanthemum Center

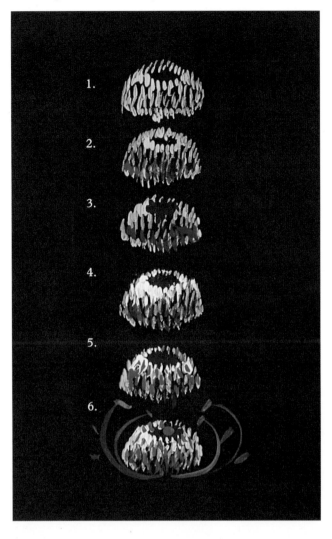

1. Use your liner tip and a dabbing technique to build a half-circle shape, leaving an open bowl in the top.

2. Begin to add contrast by adding a shadow of Alizarin Crimson around the bottom of the shape.

3. Deepen the inside of the open bowl with Payne's Gray as well as the shadow around the bottom.

4. Add highlights along the front edge of the open bowl, allowing this color to gently fade around to the sides and back.

5. Adjust the colors, adding more shadows, highlights and color as needed so that the color blends evenly.

6. Add a dot of color to the center of the open bowl. Red Light works nicely here. Add lined stamens for more interest.

The Apple

If you follow the step-by-step instructions and illustrations for the apple, you will understand the painting of the other featured fruit. Experiment with the use of added colors and reflect these colors in your leaves. Be generous with paint. Do not overblend, but rather allow the individual colors to be evident.

1 Undercoat with white.

2 Basecoat with color. Yellow mixed with Sap Green was used in this illustration.

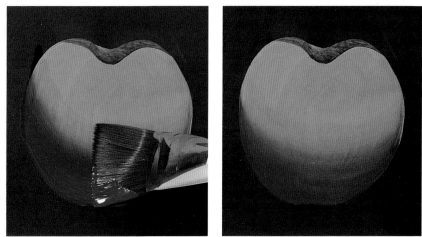

3 Use a large flat brush to float a shadow of Payne's Gray in an M shape at the top of the apple.

4 Float a significant shadow of Alizarin Crimson around the bottom of the apple.

I used acrylic paint for the first four steps because of its quick-drying characteristic. The remaining steps were done with water-soluble oil colors. These same steps could be continued in acrylics using the wet-into-wet technique.

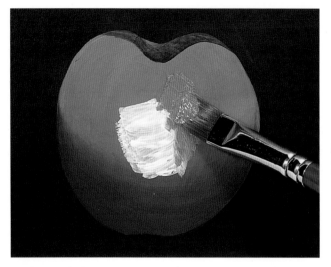

5 Begin the wet-into-wet technique. If using oils, apply a very thin, even coat of linseed oil to the apple surface. Acrylic painters should use Blending Gel Medium in a larger quantity. Place in the color, beginning with the lightest area in the middle of the apple. Gradually work out, adding deeper tones.

6 Choose a variety of colors to add to your fruit. In the photos, white, light pink, yellow, Alizarin Crimson and Sap Green were used. Payne's Gray was added to the top center stem area.

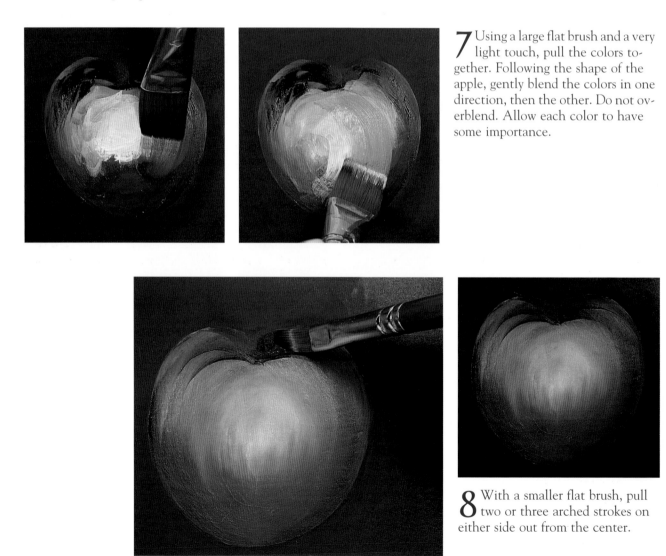

7 Using a large flat brush and a very light touch, pull the colors together. Following the shape of the apple, gently blend the colors in one direction, then the other. Do not overblend. Allow each color to have some importance.

8 With a smaller flat brush, pull two or three arched strokes on either side out from the center.

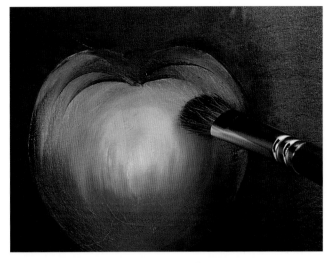

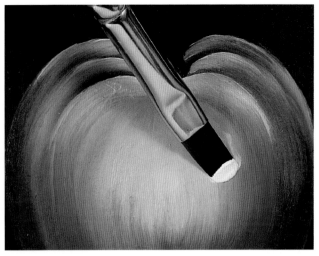

9 Use a mop brush to soften the color. Gently wisp over the painted surface, wiping any paint off of the brush and onto your soft, absorbent towel between each stroke. If you use a mop for blending acrylic paints, be sure to clean it immediately after you are done using it.

10 Use a filbert brush and short, wisped flat strokes to create additional highlights.

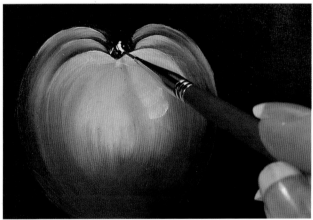

11 Add highlights by floating light color under the arched strokes of the apple, which were done in Payne's Gray.

12 With your liner brush, dab in a cluster of yellow, white, Payne's Gray and Alizarin Crimson to the center stem area.

13 When the fruit is dry, you may want to go back and glaze additional color, highlights and shadows.

The Cherry

1 Undercoat.

2 Basecoat with Red Light.

3 Add the first shadow color,
Alizarin Crimson.

4 Deepen the shadow along the bottom with Payne's Gray. Add a floated comma stroke to create the indentation for the stem.

5 Begin the wet-into-wet technique. Cover with medium. Float on highlights, heavier to one side. I added a little yellow and white to the basecoat color. Add the shadow and basecoat colors. Blend in the shape of the cherry.

6 Float additional lighter highlights under the Payne's Gray comma.

The Grapes

1 Undercoat.

2 Basecoat. Two different colors were chosen for variety—Leaf Green and Yellow Ochre.

3 Float shadows on the bottom of each grape. Alizarin Crimson was used for two of the shadows, and Payne's Gray for the other.

4 Begin the wet-into-wet technique. Cover with your medium, shadow colors and basecoat color. Add wet highlight color around the tops and slightly down the sides of each grape.

5 Blend using a flat brush, moving the paint in the round shape of the grape. Do not overblend.

6 Reinforce highlights and shadows if necessary. Add linework and a highlight touch with your filbert brush to each grape.

The Peach

1 Undercoat.

2 Basecoat.

3 Float in Alizarin Crimson shadows, and deepen them with Payne's Gray.

4 Begin the wet-into-wet technique. Lay the colors in place, beginning in the center and moving out around the peach. Highlight the top curves, being sure to emphasize the round shapes.

5 Blend with a flat brush.

6 Float highlights and reestablish shadows. Add short, wisped flat strokes for additional highlights.

The Plum

1 Undercoat.

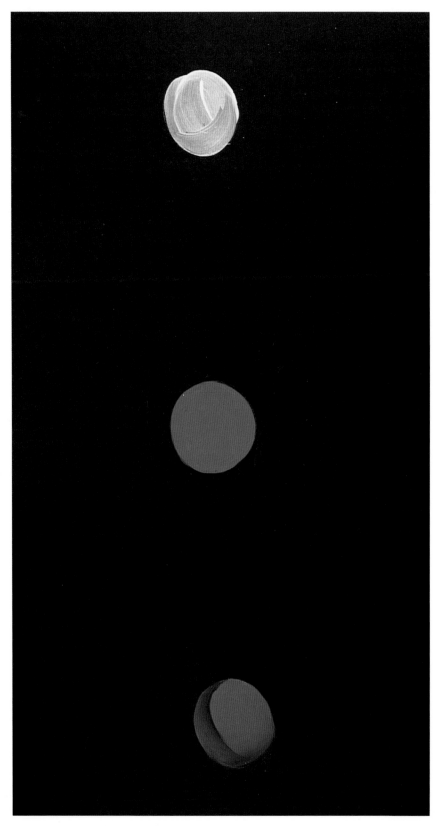

2 Basecoat. Periwinkle was used in this illustration.

3 Float in an Alizarin Crimson C stroke to create a seam in the plum. Reinforce with Payne's Gray. Add both shadow colors around the bottom.

4 Begin the wet-into-wet technique. Cover with medium. Fill in with your shadow colors and base-coat color. Highlight with white around the top and slightly down the sides.

5 Blend with a flat brush, following the shape of the plum. Finish the larger round area first, then the side crescent shape.

6 Float on further highlights and shadow colors if needed. Add a touch of highlight with your filbert brush.

CHAPTER 8
Creating Borders

Linework borders are fun, fast and easy when you approach them simply. I rarely design my border in advance of the painting. I prefer to watch it grow, and when I am satisfied that it complements my piece, then I am finished. You only need a small variety of strokes or marks and a few guidelines to be all set to create your own borders.

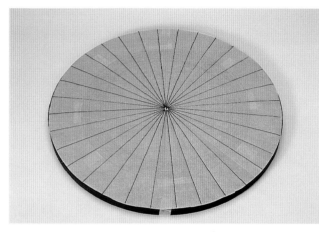

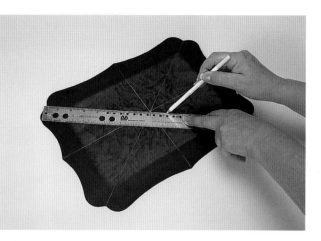

First, assemble all of the tools you will need: excellent liner brushes in three sizes (for a variety of line thicknesses), a compass, a ruler, a sharp pencil or chalk pencil, paint and medium to dilute the paint and your painted surface. In addition, a lazy Susan is handy for ease in turning your work.

Use the shape of the surface you are working on to dictate the placement of the guidelines. Draw several lines that radiate from the center of your piece to the outside edge.

Following the shape of the piece, use the compass to draw several crossing lines, varying the space between each line.

Be sure that you hold the compass straight and at a 90° angle to the piece.

Continue by working one stroke at a time.

San Diego Public Library
DATE DUE SLIP
****

Date due: 10/16/2014,23:59
Title: Just looking : essays on art

Call number: 700/UPDIKE 1989.
Item ID: 31336023234074
Date charged: 9/25/2014,14:16

Date due: 10/16/2014,23:59
Title: Stencilling on a grand
scale : using simple stenc
Call number: 745.73
 BUCKINGHAM
Item ID: 31336073487630
Date charged: 9/25/2014,14:16

Date due: 10/16/2014,23:59
Title: Decorative painting
Rostovo style
Call number: 745.723/REDICK
Item ID: 31336082295065
Date charged: 9/25/2014,14:16

Total checkouts for session:3
Total checkouts:4

<><><><><><><><><><><>
Renew at
www.sandiegolibrary.org
OR Call 619-236-5800 or
858-484-4440 and press 1
then 2 to RENEW. Your
library card is needed to
renew borrowed items.

Load your liner with paint. Choose a spot on the grid. Pick a simple stroke or shape and paint it onto the surface.

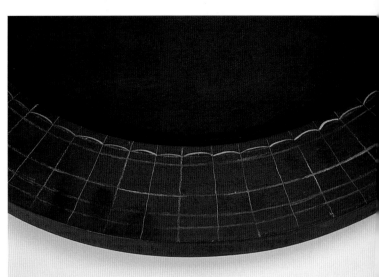

Continue to paint this same stroke to the end of the border line.

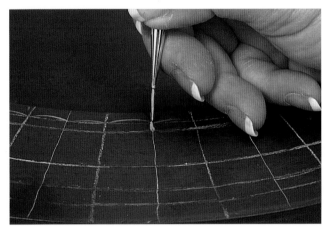

Choose a second shape or stroke and paint it anywhere on the grid.

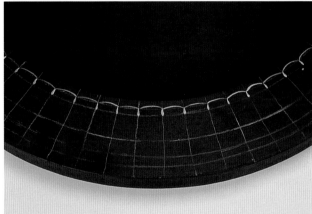

Continue to paint this same stroke to the end of the border line. As you can see, with only two simple decisions, a border has been created.

Add a third mark.

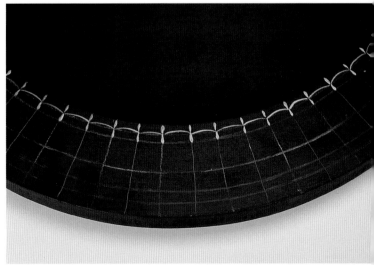

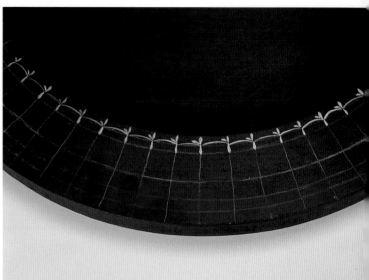

Add a fourth mark.

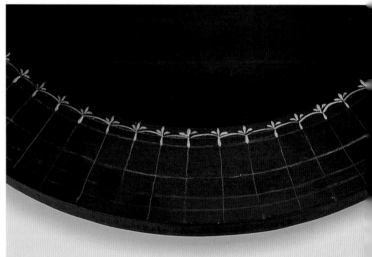

Add a fifth mark.

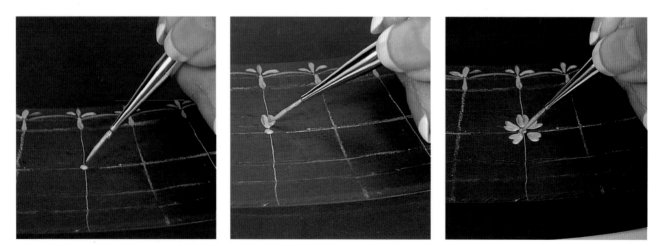

Create a "five-stroke" flower. Begin by placing a dot to mark the flower center. Pull your strokes in toward the dot. Paint additional evenly spaced flowers at intervals around the tray.

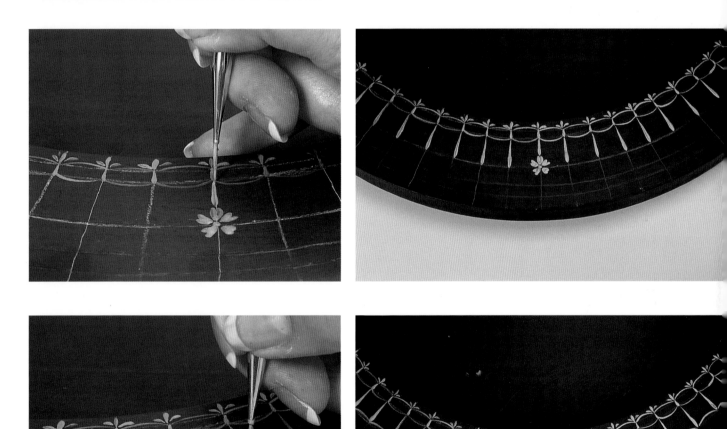

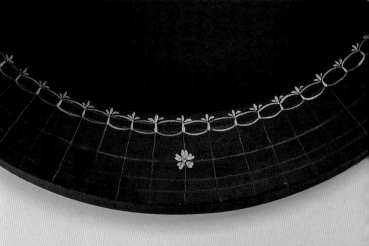

Continue working one stroke at a time.

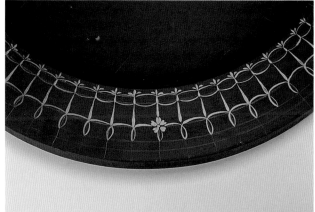

Practice to make your strokes identical. However, a little variation is expected and gives your project character.

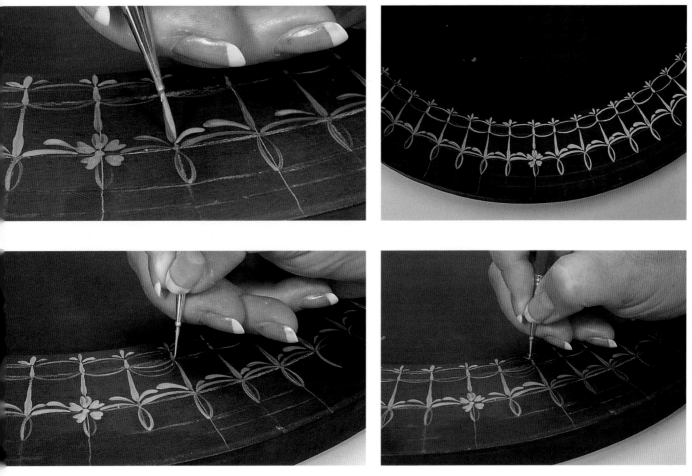

Add a pair of fine lines.

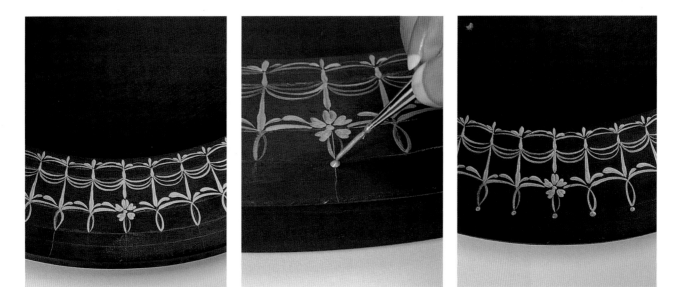

Add dots.

Continue stroke by stroke until your border is as intricate and decorative as you want it to be. Erase any guidelines that are showing.

An interesting addition to your surface may be a glass insert or cover. Approach painting borders on glass in the same manner as you would on any other surface. I add a very small amount of glass and tile medium to my paint and mix it thoroughly before beginning. Be sure to clean the glass, removing all traces of oil.

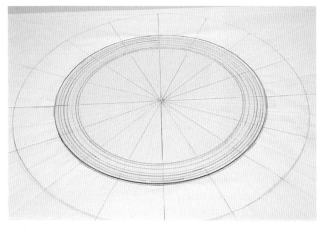

Lay the glass over a prepared grid of guidelines.

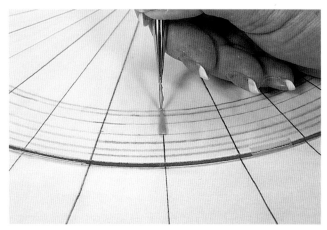

Begin with one stroke, and carefully rotate the glass to fill in your border.

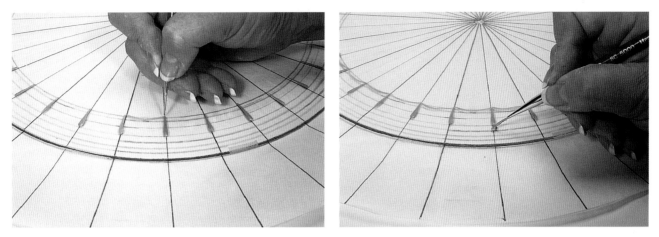

Continue to add strokes, finishing one decision on the grid before beginning another stroke.

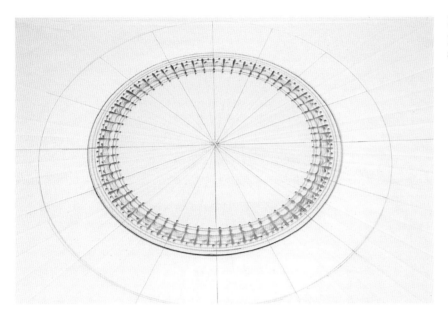

Do not remove your piece from the prepared guideline grid until you are sure that your border is complete.

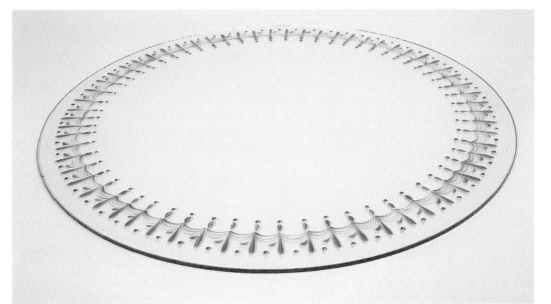

Allow for extra drying time because the paint takes longer to dry on glass.

CHAPTER 9

Glazing

Add another dimension to your finished piece by glazing the surface. Add highlights, deepen shadows and change or add colors with this easy technique.

Glazing Oils Over Oils

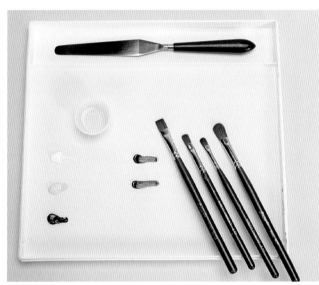

1 Prepare your palette and other necessary supplies. I gather a variety of brushes, flats and mops. I use linseed oil for my medium and a variety of oil colors. Check to see that the paint is a creamy consistency. If it is too stiff, add a drop of oil and blend it with a palette knife.

2 Cover the surface with a thin, even coat of linseed oil or painting medium.

3 Choose a color and gently brush blend it onto your piece. Alizarin Crimson was the first color used in this illustration. Before moving to the next color, mop and finish blending the first color.

4 Add a second color. I chose Prussian Blue to tie the blue background into the bouquet colors. Mop.

5 Add a third color. Mop.

6 Highlight the strokes if needed by evenly loading a small amount of white into your filbert brush and gently stroking through the medium and glazing colors.

I often use an oil glaze over my acrylic painting to give the color a boost and to add a glow that only oils can create. I used the same technique as was used for glazing oils over oils. Note that you cannot glaze acrylics over oils.

These before and after photos dramatically show how glazing enhances the look of your project.

Glazing Oils Over Acrylics

1 Cover the surface with a thin coat of linseed oil or painting medium.

2 Add your first color and mop blend. Prussian Blue was used on the flowers and leaves.

3 Add a second color and mop blend. The shadows were deepened with Alizarin Crimson.

4 Be sure to blend the colors into each other and the background.

These before and after photos show the added dimension glazing gives to your painting.

Glazing Acrylics Over Acrylics

You can glaze your surface successfully with acrylics. I use Glazing Medium and colors with the least amount of opacity. The more transparent the color, the more successful the glaze.

1 Coat the surface with a thin, even layer of medium.

2 Choose a color and blend it evenly over the areas of your choice. Yellow was used as the first glazing color to highlight both the leaves and flowers.

3 Choose a second color. Prussian Blue was used to deepen some of the shadow areas and to add another color to the painting.

CHAPTER 10

Projects

BEGINNER LEVEL

Birdhouse With Gold Leafing

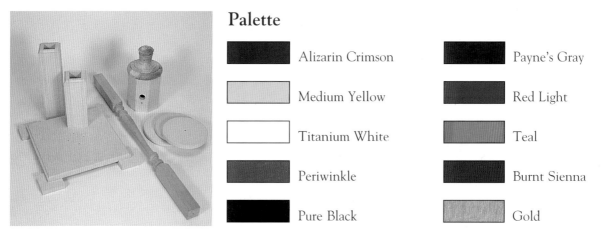

Palette

Alizarin Crimson	Payne's Gray
Medium Yellow	Red Light
Titanium White	Teal
Periwinkle	Burnt Sienna
Pure Black	Gold

Raw Surface

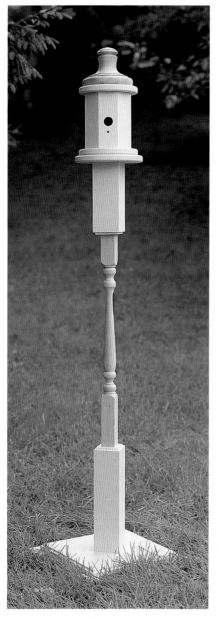

Assembled

Close-up

This pattern may be hand-traced or photocopied for personal use only.
Enlarge at 125 percent to bring it up to full size.

This border is
used on the bot-
tom section of
the birdhouse
stand.

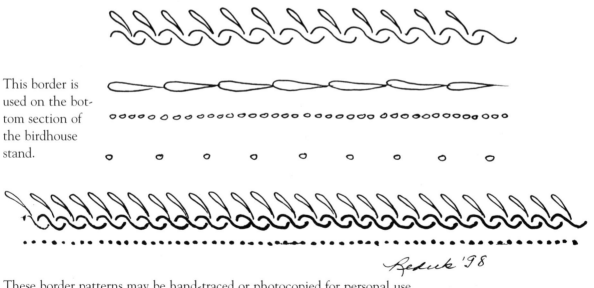

These border patterns may be hand-traced or photocopied for personal use
only; they appear here at actual size. The border directly above is used on
the middle section.

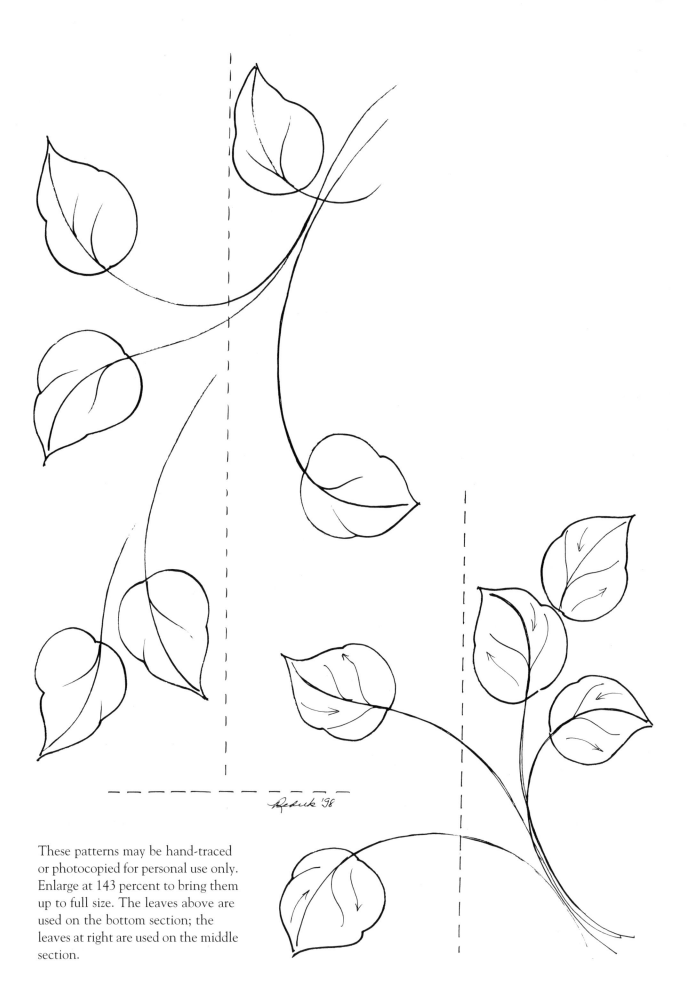

These patterns may be hand-traced
or photocopied for personal use only.
Enlarge at 143 percent to bring them
up to full size. The leaves above are
used on the bottom section; the
leaves at right are used on the middle
section.

Daisy Shadow Box

Pattern

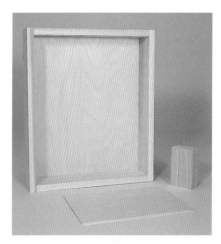

Raw Surface

Finished Painting

These patterns may be hand-traced or photocopied for personal use only. Enlarge the flowers at 122 percent to bring up to full size; the border appears here at full size.

Palette

■ Alizarin Crimson	■ Burnt Sienna	■ Light Red Oxide
■ Medium Yellow	■ Payne's Gray	■ Gold
□ Titanium White	■ Red Light	
■ Sap Green	■ Pure Black	

Chrysanthemums on Cache Box

Palette

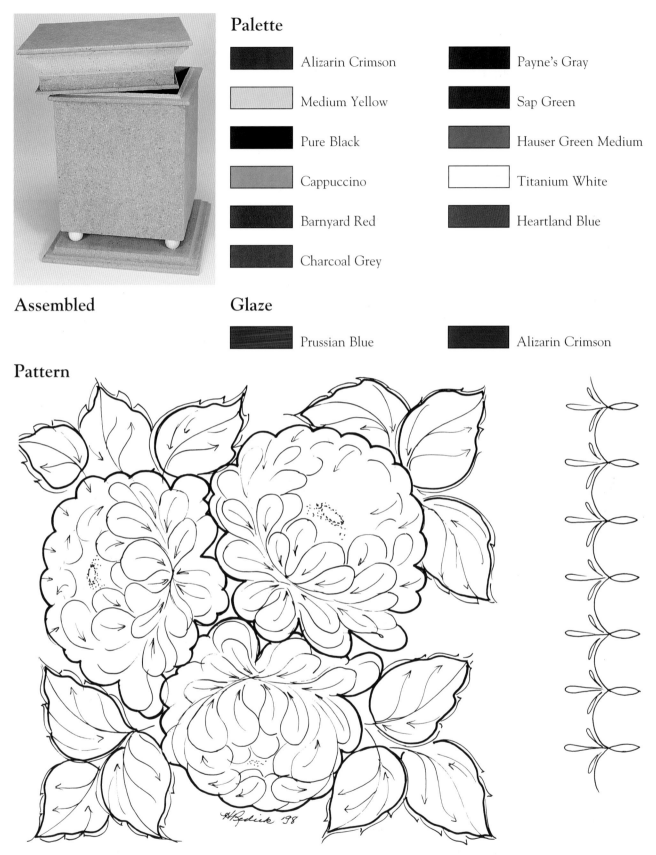

■	Alizarin Crimson	■	Payne's Gray
▢	Medium Yellow	■	Sap Green
■	Pure Black	■	Hauser Green Medium
■	Cappuccino	▢	Titanium White
■	Barnyard Red	■	Heartland Blue
■	Charcoal Grey		

Assembled

Glaze

■	Prussian Blue	■	Alizarin Crimson

Pattern

These patterns may be hand-traced or photocopied for personal use only.
Enlarge at 151 percent to bring up to full size.

Gardenia on Wedding Cake Box

Palette

- Alizarin Crimson
- Red Light
- Raw Sienna
- Sap Green
- Payne's Gray
- Pure Black
- Raspberry Sherbet
- Titanium White
- Gold
- Medium Yellow
- Periwinkle

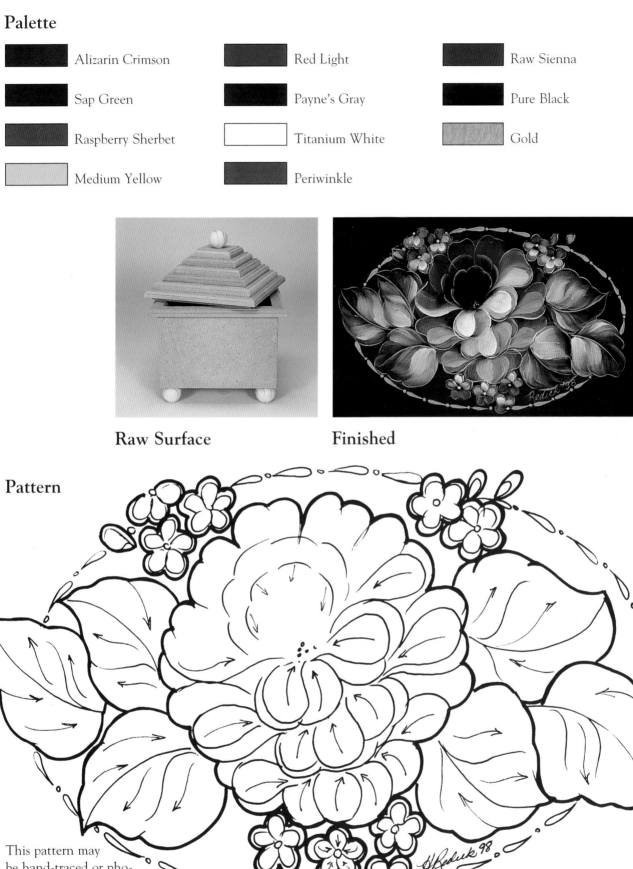

Raw Surface **Finished**

Pattern

This pattern may
be hand-traced or pho-
tocopied for personal use
only; it appears here at full size.

Floral Brooches

Palette

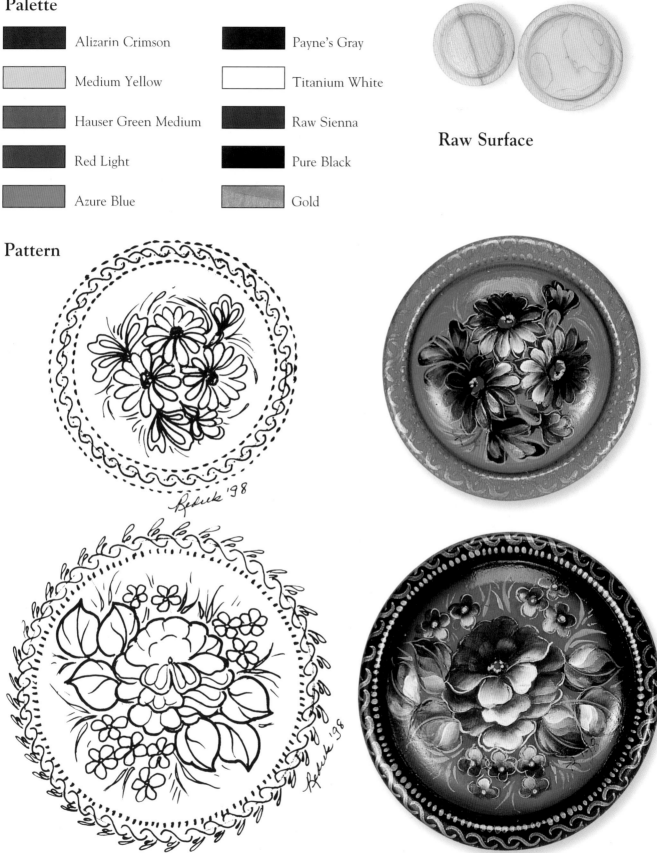

▮	Alizarin Crimson	▮	Payne's Gray
▯	Medium Yellow	▯	Titanium White
▮	Hauser Green Medium	▮	Raw Sienna
▮	Red Light	▮	Pure Black
▮	Azure Blue	▮	Gold

Raw Surface

Pattern

These patterns may be hand-traced or photocopied for personal use only; they appear here at full size.

Bouquet on Round Tray With Glass Insert and Gold Border

Pattern

This pattern may be hand-traced or photocopied for personal use only.
Enlarge at 118 percent to bring up to full size.

Palette

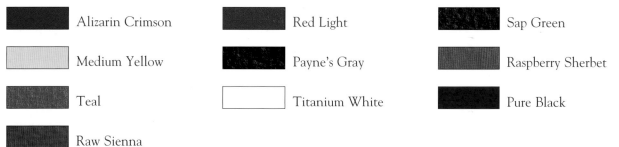

Alizarin Crimson	Red Light	Sap Green
Medium Yellow	Payne's Gray	Raspberry Sherbet
Teal	Titanium White	Pure Black
Raw Sienna		

Border
Pattern

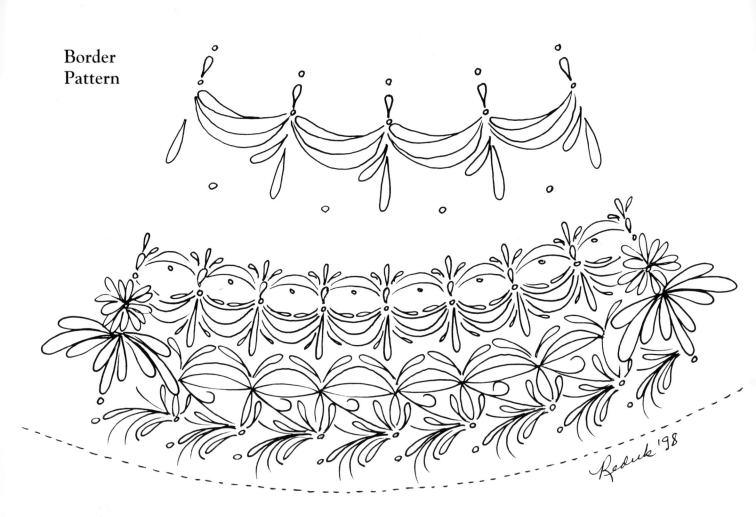

Reduk '98

This pattern may be hand-traced or
photocopied for personal use only; it
appears here at full size.

Raw Surface

Finished Painting

Chrysanthemum on Glass Ornament

Palette

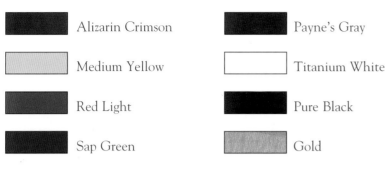

Alizarin Crimson	Payne's Gray
Medium Yellow	Titanium White
Red Light	Pure Black
Sap Green	Gold

Raw Surface

Pattern

This pattern may be hand-traced or photocopied for personal use only; it appears here at full size.

Finished Ornament

Bouquet on Metal Tray

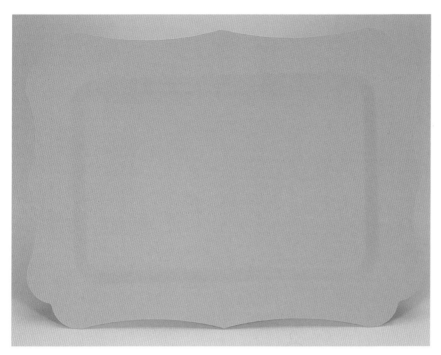

Primed Metal Tray

Palette

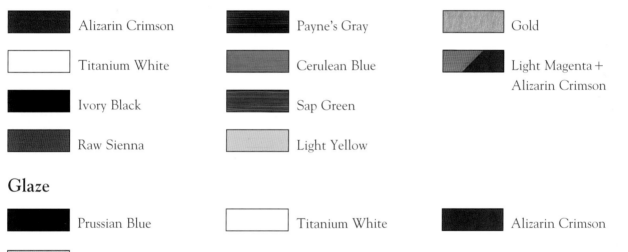

▮ Alizarin Crimson	▮ Payne's Gray	▮ Gold
▯ Titanium White	▮ Cerulean Blue	▮ Light Magenta + Alizarin Crimson
▮ Ivory Black	▮ Sap Green	
▮ Raw Sienna	▮ Light Yellow	

Glaze

▮ Prussian Blue	▯ Titanium White	▮ Alizarin Crimson
▮ Medium Yellow		

Pattern

This pattern may be hand-traced or photocopied for personal use only. Enlarge at 120 percent to bring it up to full size.

Finished Tray

Roses on Potpourri Box

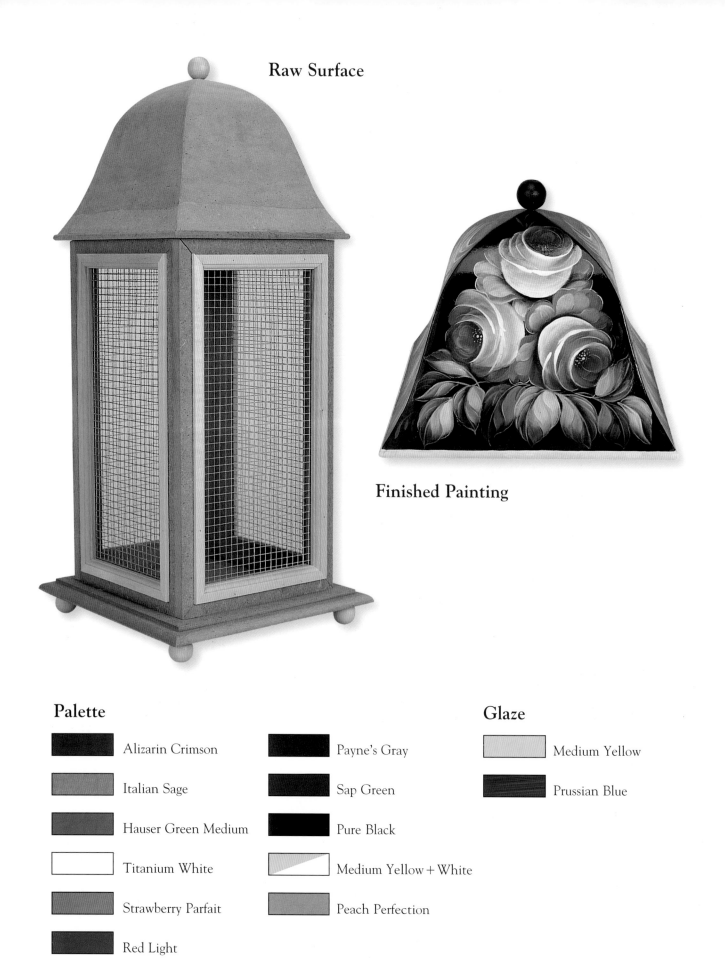

Raw Surface

Finished Painting

Palette

Alizarin Crimson

Italian Sage

Hauser Green Medium

Titanium White

Strawberry Parfait

Red Light

Payne's Gray

Sap Green

Pure Black

Medium Yellow + White

Peach Perfection

Glaze

Medium Yellow

Prussian Blue

Pattern

This pattern may be hand-traced or photocopied for personal use only; it appears here at full size.

Fruit on Pie Keeper

Palette

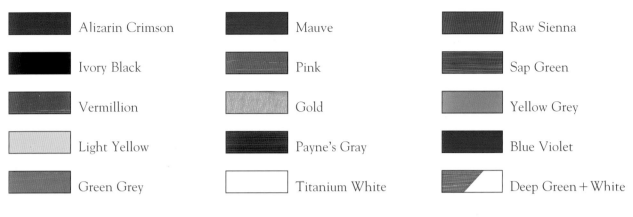

- Alizarin Crimson
- Ivory Black
- Vermillion
- Light Yellow
- Green Grey
- Mauve
- Pink
- Gold
- Payne's Gray
- Titanium White
- Raw Sienna
- Sap Green
- Yellow Grey
- Blue Violet
- Deep Green + White

Raw Surface

Finished Painting

Pattern

This pattern may be hand-traced or photocopied for personal use only. It appears here at full size; turn pattern horizontal (with apple at left) to match finished painting at right.

Finished
Painting

❧ Sources

Brushes
Robert Simmons Expression Brushes
Daler Rowney USA
2 Corporate Drive
Cranbury, NJ 08512-3604
(609) 655-5252

The Tole Booth
19 Goshen Street N.
Zurich, Ontario
Canada N0M 2T0
http://www.tolenet.com/heather

Heather Redick Liner Brushes
The Tole Booth (see above)

Paints/ Mediums
Folk Art Paints/Mediums
PLAID Enterprises
1649 International Boulevard
Norcross, GA 30093-3022
(770) 923-8200

The Tole Booth (see above)

Duo Water Soluble Oil Color/ Mediums
HK Holbein, Inc.
P.O. Box 555
20 Commerce Street
Williston, VT 05495
(800) 682-6686
http://www.holbeinhk.com

Other Supplies
Sta Wet Palettes
Masterson Art Products, Inc.
P.O. Box 10775
Glendale, AZ 85318
(602) 263-6017

The Tole Booth (see above)

Gold Leaf/ Glue
Houston Art, Inc.
10770 Moss Ridge Rd.
Houston, TX 77403-1175
(713) 462-1086

Raw Surfaces
Pedestal Bird House (page 98)
Cabin Crafters
P.O. Box 270
1225 W. First Street
Nevada, IA 50201-1555
(515) 382-5406

Shadow Box (page 102)
PCM Studios
731 Highland Avenue NE, Suite D
Atlanta, GA 30312-1425
(404) 222-0348

English Cache Box (page 104)
PCM Studios (see above)

Wedding Cake Box (page 106)
PCM Studios (see above)

Brooches (page 108)
The Tole Booth (see above)

Round Tray with Glass (page 110)
The Tole Booth (see above)

Glass Ornament (page 114)
Cabin Crafters (see above)

Chippendale Metal Tray (page 116)
Barb Watson's Brushworks
P.O. Box 1467
Moreno Valley, CA 92553
http://barbwatson.com

Potpourri Box (page 119)
PCM Studios (see above)

Metal Pie Keeper (page 122)
Stonebridge Collection
R.R. #4
2 Mill Street
Pakenham, Ontario
Canada K0A 2X0
http://www.stonebridgecoll.com

⅏ Index